PUNCTUATE IT!

END PUNCTUATION

BY KATE RIGGS

ILLUSTRATED BY RANDALL ENOS

CREATIVE EDUCATION • CREATIVE PAPERBACKS

Published by Creative Education and Creative Paperbacks
P.O. Box 227, Mankato, Minnesota 56002
Creative Education and Creative Paperbacks are
imprints of The Creative Company
www.thecreativecompany.us

Design and production by Liddy Walseth
Art direction by Rita Marshall
Printed in the United States of America

Illustrations by Randall Enos © 2016

Library of Congress Cataloging-in-Publication Data
Riggs, Kate.
End Punctuation / by Kate Riggs; illustrated by Randall Enos.
p. cm. — (Punctuate it!)
Includes bibliographical references and index.
Summary: An illustrated guide to the punctuation marks found at the
end of all sentences, including descriptions and examples of how to
properly use statements, exclamations, and questions.
ISBN 978-1-60818-733-1 (hardcover)
ISBN 978-1-62832-329-0 (pbk)
ISBN 978-1-56660-768-1 (eBook)
1. English language—Punctuation. 2. English language—Usage.
3. English language—Clauses.

PE1450.R523 2016
428.2/3—dc23 2016002551

CCSS: L.1.2; L.2.2; L.3.1, 2, 3, 4, 5; L.4. 1, 2, 3, 4; RI.3.1, 2, 7, 8; RI.4.2, 8

First Edition HC 9 8 7 6 5 4 3 2 1
First Edition PBK 9 8 7 6 5 4 3 2 1

TABLE OF CONTENTS

INTRODUCTION

IT IS LATE AT NIGHT. THE SKY IS CLEAR AND FULL OF STARS OUTSIDE YOUR TENT. THE TREES WHISPER AND WHOOSH IN THE BREEZE. DID YOU JUST HEAR SOMETHING SNAP? DON'T WORRY! IT WASN'T A BEAR! IT WAS YOUR FRIEND ROLLING ONTO SOME TWIGS. YOU CAN GO BACK TO SLEEP NOW.

MAKE IT COMPLETE

At the end of every **sentence** is a punctuation mark. A period tells you the sentence is a statement. A question mark makes you look for an answer. An exclamation point says something exciting or surprising.

All complete sentences need end punctuation. Why? This lets you know that the sentence is over! It's time to move on to the next thought. Look at the words below. Where would you break up the sentences? Which punctuation marks would you use?

I am going camping this weekend in my backpack will be a banana

You could break it many ways, but only one way makes the most sense. What if you did this?

I am going camping this weekend in my backpack. Will be a banana.

The first sentence is a complete thought, but it doesn't make much sense! However, the second

part is not even a sentence. It is a fragment. There is no **sub-ject**—it isn't about anything. How about this?

I am going camping. This weekend in my backpack will be a banana.

Once again, the first sentence is okay. This time, the second part is

a sentence. But do the two sentences make sense together? Try this:

I am going camping this weekend. In my backpack will be a banana.

With the end punctuation in the right places, now we know what's going on!

PUNCTUATION PRACTICE:

"End punctuation" means exactly what it sounds like—it shows you where a sentence ends. Where should the end punctuation go in the example below?

Hurry up all the campsites will be taken

A: Hurry up! All the campsites will be taken.

PUNCTUATION WITH PURPOSE

Most sentences end with a period. People use statements to explain what they see, do, and hear. They say where they are going. Sometimes they say why they are doing something.

I like camping because I can be outside.

You ask questions when you want to know something, right? Many questions begin with one of these words: *who, what, where, when, why, how, do, can, may,* and *is.*

***Where* is my sleeping bag?**

When you need help, get excited, or need to warn someone, you shout, or "exclaim." An exclamation point is how you write out that shout.

Look at that huge bear!

PUNCTUATION PRACTICE:

A different punctuation mark is used for statements, questions, and exclamations. Which mark goes with each of the sentences to the right?

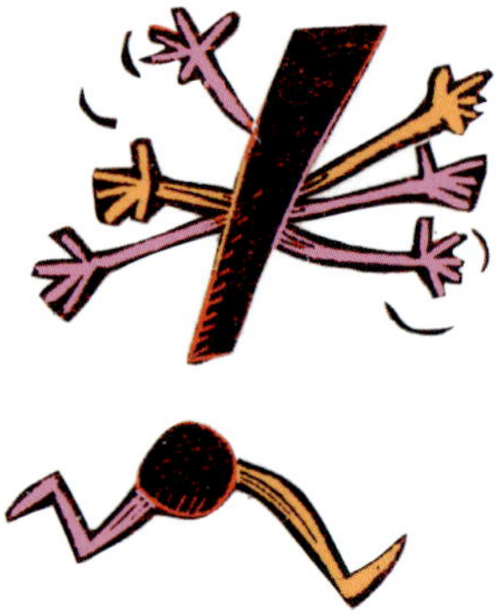

Don’t drop the canoe on me

We should hike the trail that goes around the lake

What are you doing in that tree

A: exclamation point, period, question mark

MAKING MEANING

Periods, question marks, and exclamation points act like signals. They are clues to what sentences mean. You can tell just by looking at the page if the sentence is a statement, question, or exclamation.

They also let you know how to say the words. Your voice rises and falls as you speak. It goes down during a statement. It goes up on a question word. It has a very high pitch when you get excited!

How would you say the following sentences?

My backpack is heavy.
Is my backpack heavy?
My backpack is heavy!

Look at the first and last examples again. They use exactly the same words. But the end punctuation changes the meaning. It changes how you express the idea, too. It goes from a statement of fact to an expression of pain!

PUNCTUATION PRACTICE:

End punctuation lets you know how you should say the sentence. Listen to yourself as you say these words:

The end.
The end?
The end!

CHOOSE WISELY

Every sentence comes with a choice: how will it end? Like a camping trip, a lot depends on your attitude. It may be smooth and calm like a statement.

It may be full of worry and unknowns like a question. It may be fun or scary like an exclamation. It is up to you to decide!

WHOOOO?

-ACTIVITY-

HOW DOES IT END?

You can tell a lot about how a sentence will end by looking at its beginning. Copy the words in the columns at right onto your own sheet of paper. Then draw a line between each matching pair. Check with a friend to make sure all your sentences make sense!

What color is	for your lives!
I found a cabin	will it get?
How hot	beautiful day!
Run	the bananas.
Who is going	in the woods.
What a	fast walker.
Kate will bring	the sky?
Sam is a	fishing with you?

Answers:
What color is the sky?
I found a cabin in the woods.
How hot will it get?
Run for your lives!
Who is going fishing with you?
What a beautiful day!
Kate will bring the bananas.
Sam is a fast walker.

GLOSSARY

sentence: a group of words that has a noun as the subject and a verb

subject: the noun that is what or whom the sentence is about

READ MORE

Pulver, Robin. *Punctuation Takes a Vacation*. New York: Holiday House, 2003.

Rosenthal, Amy Krouse. *Exclamation Mark*. New York: Scholastic, 2013.

WEBSITE

Grammar Blast

http://www.eduplace.com/kids/hme/k_5/grammar/

Test yourself on what you know about sentences and other punctuation.

Note: Every effort has been made to ensure that the website listed above is suitable for children, that it has educational value, and that it contains no inappropriate material. However, because of the nature of the Internet, it is impossible to guarantee that sites will remain active indefinitely or that their contents will not be altered.

INDEX